Second Harvest

Don Agey

Copyright © 2019 by Don Agey.

Library of Congress Control Number: 2019917686
ISBN: Hardcover   978-1-7960-6869-6
            Softcover   978-1-7960-6868-9
            eBook   978-1-7960-6884-9

All rights reserved. No part of this book may be reproduced or transmitted in any form or by any means, electronic or mechanical, including photocopying, recording, or by any information storage and retrieval system, without permission in writing from the copyright owner.

This is a work of fiction. Names, characters, places and incidents either are the product of the author's imagination or are used fictitiously, and any resemblance to any actual persons, living or dead, events, or locales is entirely coincidental.

Any people depicted in stock imagery provided by Getty Images are models, and such images are being used for illustrative purposes only.
Certain stock imagery © Getty Images.

Print information available on the last page.

Rev. date: 10/30/2019

To order additional copies of this book, contact:
Xlibris
1-888-795-4274
www.Xlibris.com
Orders@Xlibris.com
804783

Second Harvest

CONTENTS

Vernacular Angst 2
Retired 4
Off Track 6
What Mind?! 8
Lost n Found 10
Respite 12
Gaff Prone 14
Silly Is…. 16
Locution 18
Destiny 20
Uh, Sure!? 22
Epic Failure 24
Ouch!! 26
Kerri 28
Yucky Monday 30
Exiguous 32
Spooky House 34
Asperity 36
Rise n Shine 38
Which Road? 40
3 Months 42
Free Will 44
Looking Back 46
The Athlete's *Foot* *48*
Feign it! 50
Bumpy Road 52
Samhain 54

In Search of…	56
Party on Dude	58
Our Father	60
No Reason Really	62
Reality Check	64
Tremors	66
Quagmire	68
Unwound Journey	70
Chasing Ephemera	72
Walking With…	74
Rusty Sieve	76
Psych/ot/ic	78
Dredging	80
Heady Stew?	82
A Linear…Not	84
Thawesome!	86
From Scratch	88
Divine Aria	90
Errant	92
Quandary	94
Friday Night	96
Snooze Cycles	98
Vacuum	100
Work of Art	102
Catch-Up	104
Why Lord	106
Movin' On	108
Lottery Fever	110
Siren's Call	112
Nightmares	114
Great Expectations	116
Bumps in the Night	118
Hazy Lazy Days	120
Psalm 23	122
Arrival	124

It's Not All That 126
Extrance 128
Complex 130
A Notation 132
Pondering 134
The Light at the end 136
Cast Adrift 138
Hollow Places 140
Little Stalkers 142
A Sonnet 144
Accidence 146
A Linear Progress 148
Paradigm 150

Most of my writing experience has not been that bad; I have never thrown anything. I have, on occasion, expressed my frustration with a few colorful bits of verbiage. I admit they were both colorful and loud. At one point I did hear my cats scurry from the vicinity. Ya know, I'm not sure how well insulated the exterior walls are, or the windows. ….sigh

Vernacular Angst

I sat in this room attempting to write this
With what was a great lack of success
The whole thing approaching an abyss
And the whole structure was a real mess

The references I had could not help me
Or direct me to a reference that could
That I drank to sustain was not healthy
But it numbed what was not as it should

The words may have been tripping lightly
Out somewhere in a remote distant place
And the few that appeared were unsightly
But they quickly fled with an uppity grace

I sat in this room struggling to write this
With a small modicum of pallid success
Though my main achievement was this;
Object throwing and swearing to excess

Limerick

I walked with a guy named Larry
Had a box he toiled to carry
The bottom fell out
Stuff scattered about
The look on his face hilari – ous

Retirement is not all it's cracked up to be; It's better! If there is one word that more than defines my retirement and most of my attitude it's procrastination! Now don't get me wrong there are some things that will not be put off….but…. <u>Elan</u>; vigor, style, flair, panache (I'll let you look that one up) Execration; cursing, swearing Another little ditty about…. uh…Oh! about forgetting why I entered a room, opened a cupboard… you get the idea. There are a few scattered in this book and as I get older there may be more.

Retired

My present life has become quite the mess
And also a touch unruly
Having dumped the stress; slain the duress
It freed up a lot you see

There's much that needs doing…and I will
After the essential naps
And the reading, the vegging and I'll chill
In the occasional lapse

I toiled long at my job with verve and élan
Maybe not a lot of zeal
Work was a chore from the day it began
With no aesthetic appeal

Every new day just dragged like the rest
Except for the rare vacation
I toed the line according each one my best
And duly upheld my station

I'm ignoring the more execration prone
Work is a four - letter word
I give every praise to the title that I own
As a masterful lounge nerd

Cold Case

I entered the room with a purpose
That fled when I paid no attention
Somewhere a room with a surplus
All filed under 'Lack of Retention'

The truth is out there, but it is becoming so hard to find. Any lie, to be believable, must have a grain of truth in it to make it work. Any and every politician, and lawyer, can take a bit of truth and twist it to fit their need. The truth is so fragile and it can so easily be tweaked until it is nothing but another sound bite.

Off Track

The truth is out there
Or so I have been told
Could be foul, or fair
Something new or old

Even in the daily rags
Ones that lie the best
Look for the little tags
A hint among the jest

There buried deep inside
Might be a grain of truth
A little teaser, an aside
Could be a tad uncouth

But truth is an absolute
Both simple and direct
It's not garbled nor dilute
And is without defect

Cause it some distress
And then the truth is not
A tale that did digress
Awry from what it ought

The truth is that truth
Has a very fragile shell
Try to tweak the truth
It's all then shot to hell

Free association in rhyme. I think it's a first for me, but I don't really remember if that's the case because my mind does tend to wander and I might have written more than one. I would look through the archives, but I believe in procrastination so tomorrow will be fine, if I remember to remember to…..uh…sigh!

What Mind?!

So, how many morticians
Would it take do you think
To peel twenty-four onions
In a week, in an eye blink?

If the question you ponder
Is like the one I put down
Your mind's drifted yonder
And brain cells left town

Since I asked the question
My mind is also in doubt
So, here's a little suggestion
Open the door; let it out

Don't know what it's doing
Don't even know if it works
Not sure what it's spewing
Or how to fix all the quirks

But if I can set it straight
Set what it you might ask
A tweak to my phrenic state
And a truly ponderous task

A mind is a terrible thing
To waste and to aggravate
A wasted mind is a thing
Terrible to contemplate

It has been a while since my wife moved on to be with the Lord. Every once in a while in the peace of my loneliness a certain song, or a soft noise somewhere in the house, will remind me of something said, done or just an echo of her presence.

Lost n Found

So, once upon a time I had this nifty goal
And the means to get there
Tho' I stumbled some and it took its toll
I was on my way there

Out of the blue my goals then changed
And my focus began to shift
She entered in and our lives rearranged
And the turnaround was swift

Once I had a life to live and a place to go
And I had this nifty goal
The two of us and this new life to sow
Until they dug the hole

The first day dawned without a sun when
they brought the sorry news
Some careless hands had killed her when
Her driver had a snooze

The day she died all the life went out of a
Lost and tattered soul
Took me a while to find my way back to a
Somewhat healthy whole

Now there is just a sad and hollow peace
And a place where I abide
The Lord and friends help me find a piece
Of life at this my ebb tide

Here we have a juxtaposition if you will, or maybe not. **Respite**; taking a break from the hard never ending drudgery of the work place and **Tried**; the wanting to do something, but coming up with the uh…words on the page that have no meaning, well..they did in my head! So, there you go; a fine example of the juxta thingy.

Respite

Times where the strong
Must pause or go wrong
Let all the stresses cease
Search for some peace

Go find a good place
To rest for a space
Create a fine dream
Of a congenial theme

The burdens are there
Without thought or care
The malice is ready
The pressure is steady

So, for your own sake
Go, take a long break
You're the one owed
Then pick up the load

Tried

I try to write poetry
Full of fine verse
And end up with nothing
But learning to curse

The stuff I have written
Lies here on the page
And probably will
'til I die of old age

We all have them; the words, or the little missteps that appear without consent. I have made my share of both, or more than. Those I recognized, or had brought to my attention, I did all I could to make amends. There were a few however that I never understood as wrong and no one could convince me otherwise. Wallowing in my righteous indignation I dug in my heels and adamantly stood against the tide. In that I might have been wrong?!

Gaff Prone

Somewhere in the
passage of time
allotted to me I have
amassed a large
number of gaffs that
require
an apology. Many
are mine and
I own up to them,
but there are
some that defy my
understanding.
Where I see no
wrong, or where to
the best of my
recollection
there was no wrong
I remain recalcitrant.
Those who are in
The 'know' say,
"Apologize for it
anyway." My
response is, 'That's
not gonna happen!'
So now I'm stuck
with wingin' it
on my own and
that's really
funny! Sort of?!

Most of the time I have at least a general idea of where I'm going and what I am trying to say. 'Sometimes', a thought will pop into my head and I will follow it to whatever point it starts to make sense. I would like to say this one is a case in point, but it popped in and I followed it to its conclusion….and there you are. Make your own minds up as to what it says….I won't!

Silly Is....

So, silly can create a true balance
And sometimes it is a good thing
There are times for its allowance
And times for a sign; 'Do Not Bring'

It is the opposite side of solemn
Which is listed just below sad
Silly is niched in another column
Along with giddy, happy and glad

There're certain situations of course
Where being silly doesn't belong
Depending on the need, or recourse
Some humor couldn't be wrong

When the time and place are right
And limitations are understood
Though some ignore them in spite
Of the bounds because they could

I have tripped on the limits myself
Fueled by wine and some six-packs
Should have left it on the bar shelf
Alcohol makes any control too lax

Tho' I'm not finding any real merit
In this my inutile little discourse
Should any surface I'll then share it
It still won't mean jack of course

Every once in a while, I like to use a word that isn't often, or in this case never, used. Disedge: dis-edge; to deprive of an edge; to blunt; to dull. I found this word by accident while looking for another word and that is part of the fun. It's like finding unexpected treasure. The poem is just weird.

Locution

They all come a marching
Each rotund or slender
Crossing and/or arching
All to blend and render

Toss them into the mix
Stir them really well
Find what really clicks
And watch ideas swell

When letters do adhere
Where they are inclined
Words will all come clear
As they are aligned

Paragraphs profound
Or simply the mundane
Will then come around
Each proper or profane

Words created to be used
Documenting knowledge
Prattle has to be recused
Scatology is a sacrilege

As paragraphs abound
And stories begin to flow
One thing I have found
I can't spell worth spit

Had a 'discussion' some years ago about destiny. Is destiny some outside force that controls our whole lives, or is it a decision we make and then are too lazy to find a way out of? Immutable: unchangeable There is no destiny outside of what we create for ourselves. Like the poem says if you don't like where you are going go somewhere else.

Destiny

This thing isn't something set at birth
Or a one way only path
It doesn't move you across the earth
Or tell you when to stop

There are no ingrained genetic codes
Destroying all free will
There's no unalterable path or choice
No obligatory niche to fill

It doesn't come from an external force
But what you create within
So, you don't like your present course
Find another and go there

It is a prop and a pretty lame excuse
A delusion that's for sure
Sloth is a kind of slacker's pick destiny
That oozes a strong allure

Simple inertia was my defining force
Sloth is another word
Stuck in the rut of a dead end course
I was heading nowhere

So, go choose or allow your destiny
For better or for worse
There is one destiny for, oh, all of us
Your final ride's a hearse

In this I'm paying homage to someone I worked with. I don't know if it came from his native tongue, or that's the way he was taught English, but all conversations started in the middle, or somewhere beyond the intro. He always sounded like he was assuming that we knew what he was talking about. We didn't.

Uh, Sure!?

Don't know why it's not
Isn't that the way it's…
But then maybe I forgot
It's giving me the fits

I really thought it was
Set my calendar such
To offset this because
It changed that much

So, now I am confused
And maybe a little lost
With all the time I used
The Aspirin and the cost

I really have no idea what
This writing is all about
As I did both note and jot
The subject faded out

In case I don't remember it
Which could really happen
I will try it all again, or quit
When I am finished nappin'

If I should find the subject
Or at least a hint thereof
One thought I might inject
The one I cannot think of

I always start out with these grand plans, not always, that are supposed to lead to this one great piece that will grab everyone's focus, attention and 'jenny say qua'! That's French for, 'I don't know what'. This one comes in a close second to those I write about not being able to write. So, anyway……..that's all.

Epic Failure
Well, maybe not Epic

I searched my mind for some incredible quote
Something both pithy and profound
The world out there would laud what I wrote
And follow the skein where it wound

I'll create a prodigious exercise in epic prose
To edify, illuminate and entertain
I'll follow the tangled syntax wherever it goes
And unravel the soul of the skein

I followed the syntax wherever it pulled me
I dipped into old historical lore
At some point the search it all fooled me
I believed I was able to score

I followed all of the leads wherever they went
I was diligent and perspicacious
But it wasn't enough to 'create' even a dent
Prodigious became more pernicious

I finished with some kind of a limerick thing
With double entendre the rule
The whole thing has, like, a pedestrian ring
Anyone know of a good school?

This doesn't pertain to me, but there are a number of stories from people I have worked with. They tell a host of horror stories about their spouses and girlfriends. The more stories they tell the more I realize how lucky I was with my wife and that the prospects of doing it again are quite low.

Ouch!!

If I collected a dime
A nickel wouldn't do
To cover every time
I could pay what's due

Every time you whine
It's like grinding gears
Every nerve ground fine
And torturing my ears

And you do it every day
Tied to all the breathing
My nerve endings fray
Leaving me just seething

The pain sets in to stay
And adds a little twitch
It's a marvelous display
Doesn't miss a stitch

So doctor if you would
Please remove the pain
I'd remove her if I could
But how would I explain

Vile idea so never mind
Just a straying thought
But no other can I find
To cease the noisy rot

December 13, 1955 – December 08, 2004 I forgot to date this one so I don't know how soon, or long after she died that I wrote this. This is the first and truly the hardest. For a long time I couldn't talk about her death so I chose the only outlet I had; I wrote poetry. I'm told that eventually the pain will dim…O.K.

Kerri

December eighth; a Wednesday when I lost it all.
2004; the year's end shot to hell.
I was standing at work as my life began to fall,
in the cold and feeling very well.

The year began as years begin; celebratory eggnog
and the promise of great new year.
Ending with just pain and loss; in an abysmal fog
Just a husk now empty and sere.

I didn't know I wasn't whole until I met my wife
Then everything was changed.
But way too soon a careless hand removed her life
And my life was rearranged.

Pain and loss retain their place; now and then a tear
And the emptiness won't leave.
She carved a place in this my life and it is still here
And with every breath I grieve

God said that wherever you horde your treasure
there also you find your heart.
If I have anything adjudged of worth or measure
It's my faith, my wife; (my heart).

God said, "Lay not your treasure here on earth,
Lay up your treasure in Heaven."
I said, "Lord, all of my treasure of priceless worth
already sits with You in Heaven."

You are my heart, my life; I love you

Sitting here as a retiree it is fun to write of slave labor and long days and…you know! I look back on all the 'fun' stuff that I had to go through to get where I am now. I do miss all the ….hahaha…all of the…hahaha…no really! HaHAHA….never mind. Anyway, I put in my time and now I can wallow in the lap of…..uh..the uh…this…well, I can and I do uh…wallow…..in it!

Yucky Monday

A murky light slowly stains the horizon
With a foul shade of orange and brown
Obscuring the light that shadow relies on
And painting the day with a grungy ochre

The night and lights embellish and hide
Creating a façade of an elegant treasure
The risen sun torches the illusion to
Reveal the lie in stark and full measure

As the sun emerges people flee shelter
To wade through all the Monday muck
scurrying streets and halls helter-skelter
Dredging the septic rut that they trudge

From the gate they scatter to all corners
As the hoary day finally reaches noon
Grab any food, and drink to anesthetize
Then back to their labors way too soon

The waning hours of a moribund day
Bring thoughts of respite; the weekend
A distant dream on this yucky Monday
An ephemeral and vague remembrance

The day moves on thru the fetid smog
Which the sun relentlessly enhances
Their only goal was to reach day's end
They fled with no backward glances

As I get older the sparsity of companionship flourishes. The main problem is that as I grow older and more….uh 'mature' my heart and my mind seem truly intent on racing in the other direction. I'd say that there is a gap of about 30 years between the physical and the….. uh…'internal'? The title; 'Exiguous': Scanty, meager. There is not much more to say as the title says it all. Hair and the…..other.

Exiguous

For true love I sought
But no one was there
I looked where I ought
The cupboard was bare

So I sought others help
To create a new search
Was naught there to help
Leaving me in the lurch

As it thickens the plot
This burden that I bear
My nerves are near shot
And I'm losing my hair

To be honest and fair
On this path to true love
I'd lost most of my hair
Now it's just shiny above

The possibilities compare
To all the hair on my head
There's naught left to spare
If they haven't all fled

For true love I sought
And hope springs eternal
But what this all brought
Was an empty internal

A quiet house, book open to the good part then a sound from another room and suddenly I'm bleeding as the totally wired cats race to the source of the noise. It doesn't have to be a sound and sometimes I get a warning. A cat in my lap will suddenly tense, stare into the dark and then bolt into the other room. I love my cats, but I am not really into blood sacrifices, but who am I to hinder their passions.

Spooky House

There's a noise from an old squeaky floorboard
And then a soft sibilant sigh in the dark
Both striking an ominous and dissonant chord
Noises in the quiet unnerving and stark

Sleek silhouettes maneuver quickly in the night
As the sudden sound permeates the air
Dart into my room and the comfort of the light
Far away from the unaccustomed scare

Crouched and tense they search for the source
In the far dark niches of the house
A far-ranging search they find nothing of course
No creature stirring, not even a mouse

Just as some semblance of peace was restored
A groan erupts from a dark veiled place
The speed of the cats truly a thing to record
When they jumped with a feral grace

I think that the house has finished its settling
Poltergeists have finished their play
Now the cats can go back to their meddling
And the hunting of invisible prey

Haiku

Sleek silent shadows
Ancient armchair bleeds padding
Cat's paws need trimming

There I was, all my paraphernalia lined up and ready for the flow of what was going to be my finest work yet. Having counted every tick of the clock for a while and not a syllable visible on the virgin sheet before me it finally dawned on me that there was the possibility that I should do something else. Nap, read, stare at the clock…nap, or read…maybe a nap…..sigh!

Asperity

A tranquil room, music in the background
And beneath it the whir of a fan
Tree limbs scratch, the only other sound
Oh, my pen tapping with the fan

A desk lamp illuminates diverse idle tools
Laid out with fading expectation
Position of pencils and erasers now rules
In place of creating dissertation

Scribbles mount up on tablature margins
With a phrase or two on the page
The better stuff resides along the margins
That's more of a personal gauge

I look at this page with scribbles and all
And the paltry entries I've made
All I've accomplished is my one pizza call
And one little frustrated tirade

A tranquil room, music in the background
And beneath it the whir of a fan
Broken pencils, other stuff thrown around
And a really overflowing trashcan

haiku

green grasses reaching
orange clouds at the sun's set
black ice receding

There was a time many, many years ago when this was way too common. "I never met a drink I didn't like!"…..There was the Rusty Nail and Old English 800. They were horrible and even a man in my cups..uh.. situation could not drink them. After a while someone, more than likely God, turned off the spigot and I dried out. After all these years I still get a taste for a beer, or a mixed drink; emphasis on 'A'..One!

Rise n Shine

During the party I heard an odd buzz
Drowned out, mostly, by all the noise
And then the party began to grow fuzz
All the buzzing was dumping my poise

My eyes were losing all of their focus
And then someone turned out the lights
Did I hear someone say hocus pocus
I guess it was just one of those nights

Party was gone, but the buzzing was not
And worse, I lost all track of the singer
My head was wound in a gordian knot
And the headache was a real humdinger

I found the buzzing and it was my alarm
Which I swiftly knocked from the table
Lost in the bedsheets was my other arm
Which I searched for when I was able

The trip to the bathroom had its pitfalls
And nowhere could I find the shower
After a shower, oh and several pratfalls
Toilet and teeth then I exited the bower

Breakfast was a soggy and messy affair
And the old milk was a total surprise
Headache came back as I hit outside air
Squinted and cursed to greet the sunrise

It is amazing, if you really look at your life, just how many choices you make on a daily basis. Which road, path, do I follow and are there offramps In case that way was a bad, or just wrong, choice. In my long life, not as long as some, I have made many 'just wrong' choices and taken a few really bad onramps. My one saving grace was that I could recognize an offramp when it appeared. Anyway, life is simply a linear process. It begins at one end and ends at….the other end! What you do in between is your problem! I did my time.

Which Road?

I have pondered a lot upon several choices
Laid in a spread before me
Both pushed and pulled by disparate voices
All full of arrogant vanity

This journey having started out well enough
With a gentle linear flow
Did have its hurdles both easy and rough
But mostly an affable go

When I entered the grand world of academe
My topography changed
And when I entered the service it did seem
The whole world rearranged

Civilian life had its speedbumps and hurdles
Doors both open and shut
And then down the road when it all curdles
The pathway becomes a rut

Then out of nowhere brakes were applied
I came to a screeching halt
The atlases and rules on which I had relied
All reset to a new default

I'm now wallowing in my grand retirement
Well, maybe not wallow
Tho' I am immersed with little requirement
No paths I need to follow

I had already written the Christmas note to send with cards and I thought why not do all three. I didn't send the other two w/cards, but the idea of writing something to cover the last quarter of the year and so many fun holidays was attractive. So here they all are in their grand… finished.

3 Months

Silent shadows slide across the moon
A slight cackle can be heard
A motley crowd of creatures strewn
In a loud and raucous herd

The stampede comes to a merciful end
And a grateful quiet ensues
But Trick-or-Treat will return to rend
And to trample and abuse

- - - - - - - - - - - - - - - - - -

Drawn by the heady bouquet of a feast
I do not dawdle, or pause
I must satiate this hollow rapacious beast
One of many gaping maws

We gather with prayers of thanksgiving
For what we have received
Along with prayers of hope and forgiving
God's holy grace received

- - - - - - - - - - - - - - - - -

All the Christmas lights are hung
All the greetings sent
Toasts are made and carols sung
Candles lit for advent

God and family; friends draw near
To celebrate His day
God bless the people gathered here
And those who are away

I know that I'm deeply flawed, in fact I seem to remember writing another poem admitting that. This is hard to say, but there are things… Anyway, I have a long road to travel to get to where I need to be. Where God is waiting.

Free Will

Lord I have a prayer for You
One I struggle not to give
An ugly choice that only grew
Now burns my soul; forgive

I can't even say the word
Admit what's wrong with me
I try to hide, but it's absurd
Because what I do You see

I do not want to carry on
And wallow in this sorry sin
However my resolve is gone
I falter, fall and then give in

In the beginning it was fun
The pleasure was immense
I reserved what had begun
The addiction was intense

I'm not making any excuses
I made these choices, me
My mistakes and my abuses
Neither one comes free

Help me take this sin away
I'm yours God, but I know
I don't get to go Your way
Until I, we can make it go

Retrospection is one of the great things about retirement; it is also one of the worst things about retirement. There probably aren't very many people that want to look at some past deeds. I know I don't. Are there times in my past that I would like to go back and change? Absolutely! We all have them. Having said that…..there are way too many times back then that I would love to go back and do again; especially with what I know now…or in spite of what I know now.

Looking Back

Sitting here alone, except
for my two cats, I ponder
seventy some years.
Some years flying by, some
years crawling at a
snail's pace.
Looking back reflecting
on the good and the bad:
gaffs; silly and painful
awards; some I didn't earn.
Friends; steadfast – ephemeral,
enemies; I earned every one.
Choices that I made
and those that I didn't.
The things I had no
control over.
There are things I
should have done and
things I shouldn't have.
I survived all of it and
came away whole.
The blessings in my life:
God and
His gift; my wife
Steadfast friends
I can't leave out God's
Grace. Given to me
despite all of my flaws,
or maybe because of them.

I have been at this for a long time, mostly hit and miss with no real benefit. As I started to get serious a friend of mine told me that soon it would be like an addiction. I would not be able to go any length of time; that I would want to go. Some years later I asked him, 'So, when does the I want to do this kick in?' It has been a few years since I asked that question and I am still waiting for it to kick in. At this time I have to come to the conclusion that, that time will never occur....I lied, I'm still waiting.

The Athlete's Foot

I stepped into the sun to jog for my health
For whatever it is I have left
For years I squandered my physical wealth
There's not much left to heft

So, I stoked the old boiler for the exercise
As I stood by the couch in a trance
With too many cop-outs for me to exorcise
As my cats looked at me all askance

Yes, I hauled my old butt outside for a run
Neighborhoods for me to troll
The pace quickly changed out in the sun
And my jogging became a stroll

I stepped into the sunlight to go running
For what was to be a healthy turn
What I gained was not all that stunning
Sore feet and a slight sunburn

Limerick

His attempt to jump a hurdle
Had begun, early, to curdle
His toe clipped the bar
The fall left a scar
He's in no hurry to hurtle

There is a lot of this going on in political circles. Either they don't know what they are talking about, or they do and they just don't care as long as it fits their narrative, their agenda. I was guilty of one of their problems. I spewed things I didn't understand, but I spoke well and I sounded like I knew what I was talking about, but in the end I was called out for the pompous, and stupid, idiot that I was. It's a shame that politicians don't have those kind of people around them.

Feign it!

One should never articulate
Whatever comes to mind
Or rashly orally participate
In conversations mined

But if you elect to postulate
On stuff not understood
Learn to properly pontificate
That's speak really good

Learned that lesson long ago
via hefty foot-in-mouth
Thought I put on a great show
But it all headed south

Sometimes now I ponder first
Before it all leaks out
Not babble drivel I rehearsed
Stuff that I would spout…
~Sometimes~

Limerick

There was this fella named Logan
Lived in an abandoned Hogan
The poles rotted out
The canvas wore out
Left just his clothes and one brogan

Every journey begins with the first step. I don't remember my first step, or the first 1,000. I do remember some less than graceful steps between the first steps and now. It doesn't matter as much how many times you trip as how many times you recover. So far I've recovered one more time than I tripped so I'm ahead of the game!

Bumpy Road

The world stretches on for forever
Full of great promise and hype
With obstacles stealthy and clever
Maybe some unplanned roadblocks

Occurrences have no real reason
But do at the worst possible time
There is no obsession, or target
And as often no reason or rhyme

You must know that they will come
Come in their own time and place
There could be many, or just some
To give you one boisterous ride

Can promise and hype be the same?
They can, on occasion, or not at all
The randomness is a good fun part
The one thing; it's just not your call

They can manipulate ebb and flow
These obstacles and obstructions
They can hinder bearings you know
But it will depend a lot on the degree

I tell you now, 'Sailor take warning!'
Life will reap some kind of a toll
Your job; battening down the hatches
And getting through all of it whole

Samhain: (**sah**-win) Go figure?! Anyway, it is a Celtic festival marking the end of summer. The work was inspired by a short verse:
>'When witches go riding
>And black cats are seen
>The moon laughs and whispers
>"Tis near Halloween!"
>~ Anonymous~

It seems the older I get the more there is a 'Why am I...' in this room, or looking for something and what is it I'm looking for – sigh!

Samhain

Dark ominous clouds drifting
Across the full moon
Spelled candle smoke forming
In a portentous rune

When the world fabric rends
And the barriers thin
A fey, mystical aura ascends
A loud cackle is heard

Then dour witches go riding
And black cats are seen
The moon, laughing, whispers,
"'Tis near Halloween!"

Why am I......

I left where I was with a goal in my mind
Somewhere in transit it began to unwind
And in a very short time it all went askew
I arrived after purpose had bid an adieu

haiku

rain tapping softly
clouds cover all in shadow
shorter days ahead

It seems that the more I attempt to write the more I extrude one of these. After a while of babbling nonsense and beating myself on the head with a dictionary. I finally force some semblance of an idea, and a headache, from the vacuum that Is my thinking. Also, I do so enjoy the symbolism of soaring and fleeing.

In Search of...

I searched a while for something to write
Something to make a raucous statement
And possibly a subtly salacious slight
For some inappropriate placement

While several things did come to mind
Some that I should have kept to myself
My overworked organ began to unwind
words slipped from the verbiage shelf

It seems some scattered pieces remain
Scattered adrift in an unfettered void
Some in a swirl toward the main drain
None of them remained unalloyed

The words I could snare made no sense
All mangled and rent as they were
With but one clear word; obsolescence
Why this one's so clear I'm not sure

Nouns and verbs had fled by the score
Leaving blurry hieroglyphic grooves
Adjectives loudly out the attic door
Tumbling in some great erratic moves

Gathering momentum as they soar
Aflight in great bunches, or single file
To save them I should do a lot more
I could you know, or veg for a while

Ah, so many years, so many cheers. There were so many choices to be made in my life and way too many of them were made under the influence of beer, wine and many mixed drinks…and a lot of beer. Somewhere in the vat..uh..vast breaches of…reaches of my mind there was a sober thought waiting to break free (God is probably the one who set it free). Pondering this sober thought I deliberated mightily and came to the conclusion that I should stop….so I did.

Tout de Suite: (toot sweet) That's French for; at once, immediately

Party on Dude

I spent some warm summer nights
Dancing to a way different drummer
Parties, a lot of dancing, and fights
Drank through the long hot summer

One party drying up then shuttered
Led to my carousing at another
It was a rumor I heard quietly uttered
By this drunk's girlfriend's brother

I danced to the sun and the moon
Communed in a booze induced blur
Danced with a girl named..Maroon?
Did we dance on a table? Oh, sure!

Then, as with all things, it was ending
Summer and the parties were waning
We said good-bye by elbow bending
Lubricated, oh, every day remaining

When asked if I had a good summer
I replied tout de suite,"Yes, of course!"
It was hard to recall, what a bummer!
But I got it from a reliable source…Maureen!

Limerick

There was a couple from Boston
Walking a path they got lost on
Passed several times
The same group of mimes
Saw the same bridge they just crossed on

Admitting to myself that I have sinned and cannot let go of them is one thing, but to admit to God that I have and will continue to sin is another thing. I know that He is already aware of it. Maybe it's just that I can't admit to being that weak. I don't know how to stop. I don't want to stop.

Our Father

A prayer to You oh Father
Who was, is now, will be
From this humble author
Yes, this belongs to me

Grant me an exemption
Lord please I implore
Help me with redemption
I need that and more

See, I cannot release them
My few committed sins
Tho' I should deny them
It's a basic need that wins

So, forgive me of my sins
And several omissions
Please grant me a few wins
And proffered petitions

A plea to bring me home
I ask that You would hear
For with You I am home
And I have nothing here

Only way to Your place
Is thru the love You bear
and Your eternal grace
Lord please take me there

The title of this one should be 'Progression' as it goes from the ecstatic and hopeful to the dismal and hopeless. That is the way the progression goes on any of my poetry. Some I have had to put away for a while and then come back to. Not that it helped in some cases; one, or two I have had to put away a number of times before they actually came to fruition.

No Reason Really

This poem has a reason
This poem has a rhyme
This poem will be perfect
So crisp and so sublime

Having created a great foundation
A solid powerful start
I need a viable rousing dissertation
A tidbit from the heart

Though it has a reason
This poem done in rhyme
Neither one is working
My lack of skill's a crime

As I struggle it all seems to crumble
Leaving large gaping holes
I attempt to rhyme it and I fumble
The ball; no runs, no goals

This poem had a reason
This poem had a rhyme
But I trashed the reason
I really suck at rhyme

haiku

Soft warm sun beaming
Kaleidoscope of color
Asthma kicking in

I was never like this. I was always painfully aware of my surroundings. Most of the time I was shy with a soft blustery shell I created for protection. It was a lot later as I 'wallowed' in my own reality check that the shell became harder. I wallowed in a lot of other stuff that I won't mention here, but some of it had a unique odor…sigh!

On the other hand, I have met people in my life that were much worse than the one I wrote about here.

Reality Check

So, there was this time some years ago
When I was right more often than not
And life had a not too awesome flow
Some outcomes leaned my way...or not

So much smarter than the average bear
I'd let you know whether asked or not
If you didn't ask and I had time to spare
I'd share the éclat with which I'm fraught

I wallowed for years in this sad sophistry
Blind and oblivious to reality and fact
But slowly I emerged from this casuistry
And searched for the bodhi that I lacked

It was hard to do this cuz I sorta lost track
During the trek there was one assignation
Oops! I digress, let me get myself back
I drifted a might from my peregrination

With all said and done it was better before
When I was oblivious to the stark reality
I wasn't prepared for all the crap in store
Now I wallow more in nostalgia typically

Haiku

grey and white pallet
wind driven snow covering
vehicles; snow dunes

This one was inspired by two earthquakes that happened two days apart. The first one was on 07/04/19 @ approx. 1035 hours, 6.4, and the second was on 07/05/19 @ approx. 2030 hours, 7.1. These were far enough away that though I felt them there were no piles of books on the floor. I have lived in California my whole life and there were others where I spent a lot of time picking stuff up; stuff on the shelves and the shelves themselves. Creates a whole other sense to, 'Rock n Roll'

Tremors

There I was just sprawled out on the couch
Schmoozing with my muse
Putting cachet to the proper way to slouch
And a so-so opus to peruse

In the background the T.V. making noise
A backbeat to my sprawl
I wallowed in my torpor and a drowsy poise
Pretty much going awol

In the background I heard some rock n roll
Rhythm had a robust beat
And then the couch began to rock and roll
No rhythm shook my seat

Cats exited in a blur of black and white fur
To hide in another room
Shelves were emptied, stuff tossed for sure
One tilted shelf did loom

Eventually both cats graciously reappeared
Wove through piles of books
And while I worked at getting stuff cleared
They lay there giving me looks

Limerick

He tripped in the spiral stairwell
His fall did not bode to fair well
He missed a few steps
And rolled a few reps
His finishing dismount was swell

I have written a lot of these. At the start the thoughts and the juices flow and I get the feeling that this one will work and the inspiration will just gather and blossom straight to the denouement. All of a sudden the juices dry up and I find myself gazing at the paper with a blank stare. Inspiration turns to perspiration and the struggle begins.

>Quagmire: Awkward and/or complex
>situation; bog – you know
>bog down; sink?

Quagmire

So, my attempt at poetry
Had such a glowing start
Wasn't silly, no coquetry
experience from the heart

my true emotions flowing
by way of paper and pen
Trouble was not knowing
Would it come and when

I worked with what I had
Pushed it where I could
What output…wasn't bad
Not saying what it should

Worked well in my head
Died when put to paper
With all the reason fled
I wadded up the paper

The task I set was clear
The how to not so much
I did feel a clue was near
But it faded in the clutch

I still sit here pen in hand
Pristine paper before me
An obfuscatory mind and
A cold drink for therapy

Some one was joking the other day about entering a room and forgetting why you are there, or dialing someone on the phone and not remembering why you were calling. Well, I have done the room thing on more than one occasion so this piece was more than appropriate to write. Now if I could just remember......

Unwound Journey

I tripped on the way
to the other side
of where I was.
I'm not too sure
I was going there
from where I was
, which wasn't
where I started,
but I was pointed
in that direction so…
I started where it all
began which
was sort of funny.
Not funny in a haha
way, but more like
oh say; just strange.
Well, maybe not
strange as such, more
like leaning toward
the bizarre, or
was that bazaar?
O.K., now I've gone
and confused myself
in more ways than…
Anyway,
I arrived without a clue,
or even a hint as to
why I traveled there.
I arrived where I went
and I am still there
and I still have no clue.

A part of me thinks that having a path and fighting for it would have been the way to go, but a larger part was way too lazy to put out all of that energy. My path consisted of 'This looks good!', or drifting where the whim went. When family came along the whim went away and words like food, rent/mortgage, helter…etc. took control and my life changed forever…the change was a good thing.

Chasing Ephemera

It all started with a thing that I, well, forgot
It was a small thing at the time
Not so much forgot, I gave it little thought
It was a crimp that had no rhyme

I was on my way, obstacles weren't allowed
Goals I chased were all concrete
And those standing in my way were cowed
but it all oozed a great conceit

I was young, strong and full of…something
Never knew the words, 'Can't do!'
Pushing and fighting for some dumb thing
Always bulling my way through

My goals were all, and well within my reach
I lost track of what really mattered
When several faults became a large breech
It all collapsed frayed and tattered

What was set in stone now ephemeral; pale
Like wisps of smoke in shadow
What was clear I now saw as through a veil
I came away empty and sad so,

What was it I forgot, gave so little thought
This crimp in all my progress
From the start was me I should've sought
I was the crimp in my progress

There wasn't much of a bumpy road when I started out. I attended a semi-private and baptist school. By the time I reached the fifth grade I knew that God existed. There was no doubt. The problem surfaced later on when I decided that, O.K., God had done His part and now it was my turn to take the reins and move on. How stupid! God never walked away and I never closed the door, I just forgot He was still there. The one truly good thing I did, without even really thinking about it, was to wake up and know that He was there by my side the whole time. Thank you

Walking With...

Early on I learned that God exists
It took some time to work it out
There's also proof that He exists
For anyone who lives in doubt

There is proof in every sunrise
The blooming of spring flowers
The magic of every moon's rise
Sounds of life in the still hours

Some there are who won't believe
And others who will always doubt
Some will hate and/or deceive
And their hatred will be devout

Some there are who cannot see
And some who will just refuse
Live life as though He could be
I say, what do you have to lose?

So, whether in the quiet places
Or mired in some raucous day
God will be there matching paces
Through even the toughest day

I learned early on that He exists
I have surrendered all my doubt
I'm human and some part resists
But I still have time to work it out

I remember the first time I walked into a room and forgot why I was there……no I don't! I do remember the last time I walked into the kitchen and forgot why I was there. There was no scholarly introspection unless you count all the swearing and calling myself names. And then there is the O.C.D. If I don't put things back in the same place I will spend a great amount of time searching.

Rusty Sieve

There once was a time my mind was a trap
A vault of prime information
This prime information, both vital and scrap,
Was a part of every creation

The knowledge was there for instant recall
And it all came quickly to mind
No request made would slow down or stall
For whatever I wanted to find

A first chink in my armor came with a sigh
And a little dazed introspection
I had entered a room and forgotten why
The gap cried out for dissection

disparate info would then just disappear
And it never returned on its own
What I did remember was fuzzy, unclear,
And then like a bird it had flown

So, I had to adapt to a whole new routine
And a new set of cognitive cues
Create out of nothing a whole new scene
Filled with more than just clues

So, awash in post-it notes is now how I live
Little notes scrawled everywhere
Because like storing in an old rusty sieve
The retention just isn't there

Kitschy: Gaudy, showy and cheap.
Antiquarian: A studier of antiquities. Dealing in, or interested in Old and/or rare books.

This one was particularly fun to write for some reason. It may be that having always found psychics and fortune tellers as more entertainers and thieves leaving a little chortles at the thought of them. Are any of them real? I don't know, nor do I care.

Psych/ot/ic

She came in a cloud of too garish veils
In every shade and kitschy hue
Three sheets to the wind and full sails
This huge gaudy turban askew

She waved her hands in a careless way
While babbling atrocious verse
As she proceeded to wander and sway
The hideous rhyming grew worse

She settled in at an old kitchen table
With tarot cards and crystal ball
As she sorted, she seemed not too stable
Always on the edge of a fall

Mumbled, shuffled; dealt the cards out
Quite like an old poker dealer
She dealt the last card with a short shout
Not a shout, she's a squealer

"The Ides of March are quite certainly in
the cusp of Aquarius today."
"Never step on the back of an antiquarian,
or cross the path of a black cat!"

I left confused, but I was entertained
And short of around thirty bucks
All in all, now, I should have abstained
This waste of time really sucks

'A really itchy noise' was my euphemism for one of those nagging thoughts that hide in the back of your mind and no matter what you do it just sits there laughing at you. I have been writing poetry for a while and I can attest to it. For me it's a word, or phrase, that I know is there, but I just can't quite dislodge it. Maybe that's why the poems about writer's block have become so prevalent. Is that irony, or just twisted; writing about writer's block?

Dredging

Somewhere there's a really itchy noise
Scratching through my head
Cavorting with both balance and poise
And any composure has fled

Conducted a search for where it began
And disinterred a lot of squat
The search did create a truly good scan
Of what it clearly was not

It didn't come from any physical source
An internal, or external root
So, the only source that's left of course
Oozing from my mind, shoot!

Maybe it's just something physiological
An echo from a nasty dream
If it's more, say something psychological
My mind has burst a seam

I began this deep search for the origin
Pressure steadily mounted
I reaped nothing for all of my foragin'
Unless a headache counted

Haiku

broken fountain bleeds
ice rimmed bowl; too distant sun
scattered coins flowing

It's funny how eventually my mind drifts back to the same area. There will be a drought and then a word, or a line will pop into my head and there it is – a not so subtle allusion to a dry spell in writing.

Haiku – a ghost of a place and time – a Background to be filled in by the reader.

Heady Stew?

I began to write a poem
Full of heady thought
So pithy I would sow 'em
Both lucid and quite taut

This poem has a reason
This poem has a rhyme
This one will be perfect
So crisp and so sublime

I'm toiling on the reason
Searching for the rhyme
There was a little teasin'
A little hint of rhyme

This poem had a reason
And some kind of rhyme
I lost track of any reason
Not sure about the rhyme

This poem has no reason
I never found the rhyme
And now my brain is easin'
Into some hard downtime

haiku

Wind moans in the eaves
Shutters bang a random beat
Deck chairs are missing

Linear: in this case it's a line, a straight path with a beginning and an end. When you add the human equation it can become all curly and labyrinthine. There could be offramps that go nowhere and some bumpy turnouts. I have had my share, but there are those who have had much worse. I got through it all and survived. I only hope that I learned from all of it. I'm not really all that swift on the uptake, or the sharpest knife in the sheath, but a good thump, or a few, will get my attention.

A Linear...Not

Travelling life's sometimes rocky road
With the occasional pothole
Can be, for some, a tough heavy load
Plus the possible sinkhole

Choices I made, the jobs I didn't score
Create some of my potholes
Losing my wife when beginning to soar
One of my major sinkholes

This routing is simply a linear process
It begins and then it ends
The timeline has no pause, or recess
Or any other slowing trends

We create the problems and potholes
But light on the learning curve
So, a smarter set of directional goals
Would so much better serve

Limerick

There once was a girl named Mary
Who wore a wig that was scary
She tripped on the stair
And dislodged her hair
Now Franklin's statue's quite hairy

Aaahhhh spring! You are so welcome! I prefer early and mid spring. My favorite time of the year. Maybe you still have to wear a coat, or a light sweater, but the trees are budding and the birds are back singing; clouds glide caressing the sky. Sigh!

I drove big rigs for 6 years and I knew; I Knew, that at some point I would be unloading and I would spill something! Especially a dolly of engine oil, but to my great surprise I managed not to the whole 6 years.

Thawesome!

The too distant sun had risen as it ought
But winter still held sway
What little warmth the sun had brought
The winter washed away

A blanket of white enveloped the world
The snow still coming down
Lingering leaves lay brittle and curled
A gray and dingy brown

The mantle marred by ploughs and people
Moving through the day
Muffled bells from the old church steeple
Bless them on their way

The sun having wrapped its southerly ride
Turns for another round
Drives the cold before it on a warming tide
thawing northern ground

The snow becomes warm spring showers
And the mantle disappears
What hold that ole Jack Frost had sours
A burgeoning spring appears

Limerick

All of the stuff John was haulin'
Had a large penchant for fallin'
Stuff hit the floor hard
Left nothin' but shard
The urge to retire came callin'

Scenario: A barn with cows and horses in stalls and wandering down the aisle. You enter the barn leaving the door open and while you are trying to do your job they just wander out. You manage to hold onto some of them, but when you turn your back they leave. Sometimes when I am trying to write it feels just like that. I do, in the end, create work, but I really hate wandering in the large empty echoing spaces of my mind.

From Scratch

Thoughts arrive both wan and pale
As shadows in the mind
Filtered through some tattered veil
It made them hard to find

Scattered thoughts accumulate
In places too obscure
Hard to find and contemplate
With all becoming fewer

Dredging words that won't be found
To pull them from their place
Running errant thoughts to ground
Before they self erase

First I had to search a mind
That's pretty much unmanned
Tools there were hard to find
To do the job at hand

Once there was a place to work
And proper tools found
Waded through the sludge and murk
To write the not profound

Thoughts did trickle in this drought
Some managed to adhere
Making sense of what came out
Will take time I fear

Have you ever awakened in the morning and in the peace just before rising, well, maybe not in the city, but away from the noise and conflagration that is the city, if you are quiet there is something in the stillness that almost sings. O.K., maybe you don't, but it is there and I am not delusional. Maybe you just need some training in listening. Of course, living in the city and the sirens going off as the sheriffs raid the apartment complex across the street it is hard to hear.

Divine Aria

In that small hush when night and day
Juxtapose
Listen and you might hear some stray
Epic prose

The song God wrote to honor all He
Had created
A song of love from the Father to be
Celebrated

It sings through the heart and the soul
Exhilarating
The daily grind can muffle the whole
Hearing thing

Assailed daily by loud adverse noise
We are inundated
Our hearing, cogitation and yes poise
Incapacitated

So, find a quiet moment in the day for
Listening
A calming time away from the fray for
Your thing

Rose 3

Some roses are red for a reason
And violets have a dark rich hue
No matter the time, or season
My love's in full bloom for you

Every so often I write some little ditty and want to share it. In the case of the haiku, that's as good as it gets….oh, and also the limerick. So, if you are reading these and something sounds, I don't know, off? It is. If you are reading the regular poetry and something sounds familiar; well what can I tell you? I write what comes to mind and sometimes I head in the same direction.

Errant

Deep into my life I found
One day
A small snarky path weaving
Its way
"Come follow", it called, "every
Small bend."
I'll follow this track right to
The end

Limerick

I once knew this dude named Gary
Married a girl down from Derry
She ran him to ground
His bruises abound
Her game plan really quite scary

So Retired

The choice to retire was so rudely set
When I went left and my knee went right
I cannot pretend there was any regret
The thought itself was too heady

Now wholly ensconced in a better career
I can wallow in a whole lot of new choices
To do, or not do my choices are clear
And my course ahead is steady

Oh, those wonderful day jobs; 0900 – 1700! Or what ever covered the 8, or 9, hour work day. I have heard that eight-hour days have become the exception rather than the rule. My days, before I retired, were never 8 hour days. They were more like; 2300 – 0800, or 2215 – 0700hrs., or longer many times. 12, 13, 15 hours were more my norm. You want to talk about culture crash I went from two hundred miles per hour to four…really nice!!

Quandary

In the evening as peace envelops the night
When the noise and distractions are gone
Then I can see through the eyes of hindsight
What was clear and what sketchily drawn

Was this choice needed, did that one work?
Did I cause pain, or discord to any but me?
Were there other options and did I so shirk
My obligations, or maybe I just didn't see?

Just as the day dawns there is incoming flack
Decisions, distractions abounding for hours
No chance to think, only time to fight back
What breaks we had were not really ours

Did the frantic decisions lead to a solution?
Were they a bane, or boon to the progress,
Or did they cause some obscure dilution?
Oh, for a vacuous and protracted recess

The peace at night though was truly fragile
Subject to the whims of feline roommates
I endeavored amidst the stealthy and agile
But left scratched conclusions to their fates

Though humbled and flawed to a degree
I try to be honest with myself; more, or less
And try to learn from those choices, maybe
How well I've succeeded is anyone's guess

I stayed in the college dorm my first year of academia. It could just as well be the daily life of a fraternity. Either way there is a striking similarity though the dorm may be the more subdued of the two.

Inutile: of no use, or service

Friday Night

Raucous noises echo up and down the hall
And thin walls vibrate in response
Amidst the cacophony is a scatological call
And slews of lewd and bawdy replies

The hallways cluttered with pungent debris
Damp from, 'I do not want to know!'
A large pile of scree seems to be breathing
With a loud, snorting irregular flow

Yes apt. 3-F way down the hall is the source
Of all that is sticky, potent and loud
Yes they are extoling the weekend of course
The one they won't really remember

For those who would rather peace and quiet
I wish you both blessings and luck
Because barring any real intervention here
You are well mired and truly stuck

Inutile

I pondered both long and quite hard
On nothing of any real merit
Or truly nothing I can't just discard

My aid during work was a fine claret
It is held in such high regard
Now it's empty I really can't bear it

Oh wait, I still have a six pack, I do!

Lately, since I retired, my sleep has been more a series of episodes than one long documentary. During the commercials I will, on occasion, hear a few thumps as my cats try to open the hallway cabinet, or the occasional dispute over……? Also, during the commercial I will have the remnants of something that I was dreaming about and no matter what I do it fades, and I am stuck with an ephemeral tease.

Snooze Cycles

I rise in the early
morning hours, for
the third time, and
sit on the edge of
the bed listening
to the sounds of
the house.
The creaking and
complaining of a
forty year old house;
the bangs in the
kitchen as my two
cats attempt to open
cupboards.
There is a kind of
peace in all of this
as I sit and ponder
yet again for the
umpteenth time an
as yet unanswerable
conundrum.
Now if only I could
remember what it
was that was so clear
earlier, twice, then
faded. If not, maybe
a good definition of
conundrum.
…or maybe I could
change the rule and
the fourth time is the
charm.??

Ah, poised on the brink of excellence with scribe thingy in hand and the overflow of…of…O.K., so there isn't even a trickle, so what's your… my., point? That is my point! I sit there surrounded by all this crap and the best I can do is doodle a cat. It doesn't look like a cat, but….it's what I doodled. I guess I could sharpen the pencils again.

Tick tock, tick tock….LEAVE ME ALONE!!

Vacuum

Old mellow music and a fluorescent light
Caress the white vellum tablet
Typewriter, with pencils and erasers alight,
Plugged into an overwhelmed outlet

References and thesau..ruses..rai? abound
To facilitate my best effort
A few how-tos for Dummies are around
To which I just might resort

I'm squared to the desk awaiting the fight
Fingers beat a martial tatoo
I searched long, but naught came to light
But the many lost hours I rue

The pencils and erasers I again rearrange
Offer no help in my case
As my mind wanders to some place strange
I stare into a vacuum of space

Soft mellow music and a pencil held high
A pristine tablet of white
I hover with the pencil and ready to scry
As though I actually might

Limerick

I heard this one politician
Bragged he was truly patrician
Glissade missed a stair
His head bounced a pair
Finished in a sprawled position

I was blessed with a lot of charismatic women in my life; both in the work place and out. Beautiful, skilled and talented women who made being there a lot more enjoyable than would otherwise be so. I must give equal comment to the other side so; they had their moments. So, as I was saying about the beautiful women in my life….thank you.

Work of Art

She walks with grace and elegance
Each step a work of art
Eyes are drawn with but a glance
To linger and to chart

Her form is sculpted to perfection
Such a classic shape
I have so far escaped detection
Standing all agape

Each day with her is such a gift
To hear her speak a joy
Her every smile gives me a lift
I feel like such a boy

Each day it gets a little warmer
She is just so hot
I spend the day just gazing at her
Hope I don't get caught

I must admit I've been consumed
By everything I've seen
And my heart has been assumed
By her passionate mien

I would like her in my life forever
But not a good idea
Cuz' office dating, or whatever
Not so good so see ya'

I was never one of those who saw their value through the eyes of others. Then again that wasn't always true. There were times in my younger life wanting to be accepted into a certain crowd. On the other hand I didn't try all that hard either because it seemed like a lot of work for little reward. Then I became comfortable in my own skin and it was all copasetic.

Catch-Up

Yes, I looked, but I did not see
What others saw so clear
And yes, I listened occasionally
But never learned to hear

For all the knowledge to be had
And not too hard to find
My lack of interest was so bad,
And a fairly porous mind

So, much later when I woke up
I took a slow look around
And I found a way to catch up
With bodhi that I found

Awash in all of this knowledge
And still somehow behind
Has forced me to acknowledge
I might just stay behind

If that's the way it will turn out
I'm fine with what it is
I can stop it before I burn out
And become a trivia whiz

haiku

leaves dance in the wind
clouds herded across the sky
one missing trash can

It's not that I want Him to map out my future for me, though I do, but is it so bad to ask for a hint, a suggestion? I'm getting older and tired of all the bumps in the road and the obstacles that I don't know how to handle. So, during a prayer when I'm asking a question maybe a whispered yes or no, or even a snicker would point me somewhere.

Why Lord

Lord, please allow me one small clue
For support and to sustain
Even the smallest of hints would do
To explain why I remain

I now wander through it all alone
No direction and no goal
This flawed bit of flesh and bone
And a weary battered soul

There was a time I had a reason
One tangible and here
Guiding me through every season
Now frangible; unclear

She made my tattered life complete
Scattered pieces whole
With her gone there's just defeat
A large and gaping hole

I've been told that You have a plan
For every one of us
To have a plan for this one old man
Would surely be a plus

So I'm scanning for a simple answer
For a simple yes, or no
It's Your timeline and Your plan Sir
Maybe just a hint or so

This one was fun to write. Stuff popped into my head and it worked for the poem. I did this one in record time, for me, and there was no staring into space, or doing a crossword puzzle...or doodling! O.K., first: *Tule*(too-lee): either of two large bulrushes usually found in low lying land and marshes.
Zilch: zero, nada, nothing

Movin' On

Life began in a small valley town
Buried in some cold tule fog
Winters cold, wet, gray and brown
Could only be loved by a frog

Teeming masses and truly diverse
Urban, suburban and rural
I was raised in this wee universe
Nurturing what would unfurl

Volunteered for the service then
And followed one simple road
It all changed at the point when
I entered the civilian mode

The path up ahead kept dividing
With an annoying regularity
And all my choices kept colliding
With a confusing singularity

With good choices following bad
And others I...never mind!
Were there better choices I had?
Zilch there I wanted to find

Now my road is simple and clear
Fewer unexpected diversions
Retired, I revel in each new year
And 'Never mind!' excursions

I didn't play the lottery for the longest, or anyway, for a long time. Now that I'm playing I'm afraid to stop because I know that when I stop my numbers will come up and I will have blown all that money for nothing. There is always the surety that the numbers are coming up and just around the corner - - Sucker!

Lottery Fever

Twenty times say twenty times
I have played the lotto
And for at least that many times
I have come up blotto

For those of you the educated
Blotto means I lost
But those of us the dedicated
Never count the cost

I look for the winning numbers
And the mega one
My jaded life plan slumbers
Waiting for,"I Won!"

So we rob Peter, oh and Paul
Just so we can play
Maybe not the smartest call
Nor logical I'd say

I've been teased a time or two
By some little wins
Ones and twos and such won't do
Cuz poverty begins

But I cannot stop, nor will I stop
I know my win is soon
The numbers that I need will drop
Or poverty is soon

Ah, the rigors of retirement. All of those difficult and important decisions to make and the effort, the energy expended, made to reach the proper conclusion. The distance from the couch to the fridge was, maybe, 10 – 12 feet and the distance from the couch to the bathroom was, drum roll, exponentially longer. What finally propelled me from my preferred position was simply a 'pressing need' - - so to speak!

Siren's Call

I can observe that gleaming grey storage unit
From my fine strategic post
That hum from the fridge calls me to use it
The pulling has me engrossed

From my couch I contemplate possible need
And the chance of withdrawal
Or the chance I would become weak kneed
And buckle at this siren's call

I kind of cringe at all the effort it would take
To move me from here to there
I have to consider the long distance to make
And all of that…wear and tear

Which is more pressing this far in the game
The fridge, or my planted butt
A debate is too taxing and coming up lame
So, I'll take a hint from my gut

In the end what drove me was simply need
A hunger that began to loom
Arrive at the fridge before IT began to feed
And a raging need for a restroom

Limerick

He tripped in the spiral stairwell
His fall did not bode to fair well
He missed a few steps
And rolled a few reps
His finishing dismount was swell

I've never had that many nightmares, but there are people I know who have a lot more and remember them. I don't remember dreams except for little bits at the end as I wake up. There are nights when I don't sleep as well as others so maybe…hmmm!?!?

Nightmares

I'm lost somewhere that's really dark
With naught to light my way
Along with things of a feral mien
And something very fey

Shadows flit and flow from sight
Yet always hover near
A dark and angry, hungry night
I just might be the food

Rippling light from far above
In all the shades of blue
I struggle to attain the surface
But I'm never able to

The desert stretches far and wide
The sun is overhead
I face a vast forbidding space
Alone among the dead

I wake up to the sound of oldies
And sweating like a pig
Harsh and jarring sort of trauma
Does both pry and dig

When I rise dip turns to sway
My eyes a foggy blur
To greet a long and ugly day
I really need coffee

These are appearing way too often. I try to write something of merit and end up whining uh…writing about the fact that I can't. I need to …uh…re…sigh!

    Limerick: Clowder; a group of cats!
        Askance; look at w/suspicion, or disapproval

Great Expectations

I was filled with the great intention
Of writing a marvelous tome
The fault was my lack of retention
And my mind tending to roam

The Bard was my grand inspiration
I expected the words to just flow
All the hard work and perspiration
And the long-awaited flow was no go

So, all the equipment was ready
Like erasers and pencils and such
My head and hand were both steady
I had the Bard's work as a crutch

With paper before me I put pen to
Hand and…. doodled a flower; nice
And a penguin, then a kangaroo
I sketched both of my cats; twice

I was filled with the great intention
Of writing a marvelous tome
But due to some stray intervention
All I got was this short silly pome..uh…poem

Limerick

The clowder in a real hurry
Raced to the room in a scurry
They all looked askance
the chair stood no chance
poor chair all shredded and furry

Halloween has always been a fun time to write about. There is always so much going on with the myths and the history; and all of those children scattered through the community with their costumes and bags for candy. I wrote this one years ago for my wife. We were apart around that time for a few months trying to buy a new, for us, house (the house was built in 1907).

Bumps in the Night

Goblins and ghouls go bump in the night
Abroad on their annual hunt
A mixture of creatures horrific of sight
Loud and raucous and blunt

These spirits are driven to ravage and seek
Aflame with a hunger and more
Mere mortals flee from the havoc they wreak
In their flight to be first to the door

Poltergeists scurry and screech in the night
Goblins just trash everything
Witches dance frenzied in the moon's frigid light
Ghouls do more of a fling

They all are the owners of All Hallows Eve
These creatures of myriad shape
As scary a scourge as one could conceive
One truly phantasmal landscape

But all too soon their reign will subside
They'll have to abandon the night
Retreat from morn's light; there to abide
Until the next hallowed rite

haiku

small creatures darting
careening through light and dark
bright flashlights bobbing

I finished this around the same time as I retired. If I had waited to write this one I would have crafted a different poem. Yes, there is some down time and I will admit to some vegging, but that can only get you so far and then you have to find something. In my case I have time with friends, write, clean the house…uh..go to the gym and take some time for re.a..d…i….n…….gzzzzz

Hazy Lazy Days

Time drifts away in the background
A vaguely noticeable blur
No anchor to mark time was found
Nor did ought of note occur

A vague something almost appeared
Of the fuzzy obdurate kind
But overwhelmed it then disappeared
Into the ooze of my mind

The sameness has a certain flavor
A slight bitter aftertaste
A sameness that's easy to savor
Nothing to be embraced

I suppose that there might be some
Draped on a couch somewhere
Who would relish the stupor to come
With a glazed and empty stare

Inertia when left to its own devices
Generates more of the same
Should be high on the listed vices
Addictive and totally lame

Time drifts away in the background
As I search for something to do
There were some things that I found
As I nodded off in the loo

Much of this poem just says cut right to the point. There is nothing here for me. So, if You're done with me please just Let me go. I know I'm flawed, maybe flawed beyond redemption, but I've tried the best with what I have – please let me come home.

Psalm 23

The Lord, He is my Shepard
I've so often read, so
Where is it He would herd
Me; do I want to go?

Please Lord, if You're guiding
Guide me to the light
For I'm here and now abiding
In deepest darkest night

He leads me beside still waters
Another life and time
But life's ugly churning waters
Is where I do my time

Lord please I need to ask you
If You are done with me
Am I finished, if I am through
Please Lord set me free

I yearn for Your green pastures
And still waters so
As one of Your own creatures
Please, just let me go

Of course my life is by Your will
And everlasting Grace
So let this humble life be still
With what sorry grace

At the beginning of my retirement there was a lot of introspection. No there was not! There was a little at one time or another, but I was (am) too busy wallowing in it to think about the past. There was this one woman that I.......never mind!!

The more I wallo.....uh delve into being retired the more I thank the past for getting me here and in this condition, but I'm not going to flounder in things gone by. I'm going to look to the future and all that's waiting for me to screw it...delve!

Arrival

There was a time not so long ago when I had a hold on my life. Transient and frangible It wasn't a strong grip and there were times when I fell, or lost my grip. There were a few times when I just let go and gave up. It doesn't matter how many times you fail; what matters is how many times you get up and start again. At one point it took a long time before I got back up…but I did. Times change and now there is a whole lot less to hold onto. I don't have to hold on so tight either. For 55 years I toed the line and did the work. Now it is my time and the clock is just a piece of tick-tock noise on the wall. I even learned how to spell procrastination.

Some people plan for retirement on the first day on their first job. Some get down the path of life and start to plan. Then there are those, like me, that are pushed into retirement on a second's notice and have no clue about it. Here I was just cruizin' at work, quickly, when I torked my knee and my career was over. It started with fighting with worker's comp. At first they refused surgery and then, reluctantly, complied. At the same time trudging my way through Social Security and medicare. I was retired for 6 months before I could actually enjoy it.

It's Not All That

Images are scrolling across the screen
Alternating dark and light
Repeated images I've too often seen
Help me through the night

Some little noise from another room
Piques the cats' regard
On the T.V. there's a baritone boom
From some electronic bard

There is more time for noticing now
All the sounds of the house
And, also more time for ambling now
Amidst the stuff in the house

I walk through the gathered treasure
Accumulated over the years
I've done well by anyone's measure
Through too many careers

I had made no plans to stop working
Or created a plan to retire
A part of my body stopped working
And I was forced to retire

Now, late at night I can hear a clock
Marking the passing of time
So much time between tick and tock
Muddling my internal rhyme

So, to the title first. I saw this on a door one night while I was at work. Not exit, no entrance. When I was about half way through this the sign came to mind. I wasn't sure where this poem was going when I started, but I finally found a direction, a purpose of sorts. I would rather not come back as a cow to be eaten unless it's an east India cow to be worshipped.

Extrance

Several things have come to mind
Concerning the afterlife
There are no facts that I could find
Several rumors are rife

No facts discovered in my search
And no witnesses exist
The lack has left me in the lurch
No evidence to assist

There are those who say there's none
At the end you are through
Some others who say life's just begun
So careful what you do

Yet others suggest that we come back
Not necessarily as a human
With all of the choices there to track
The choice is up to you man…..or woman

Does life revolve in a large turnstile
Or a simple one way door?
Is our final exit a long slow single file
Out to the trash compactor?

I will post a question now for you
It's a simple one; 'what if?'
What if this afterlife thing is true
should you model life, 'as if'?

An homage to the tragic liberal left. They spew loud and terrible sound bites meant to frighten the ignorant and the weak. I have watched them as they ride their rhetoric, unfounded and lacking facts, to a foregone conclusion that isn't. I wish them well, but I pray that they fail and not take this country and flush it down the toilet. A more devastating direction I cannot conceive.

Complex

I stare out in perplexity
At a myriad of hands
All waving in complexity
Obfuscatory strands

So, are they celebrating
In their ebb and flow
Or are they deliberating
On some sorry show

Words echo intractability
Battered by rebound
They lack some flexibility
As the words resound

There's some deliberation
Over what it is about
And there is consideration
On just why they shout

Words fragment combustibly
Scattered to the wind
Meaning lost irretrievably
No ability to rescind

In the end it was irrelevant
Topic long forgotten
Volume was more relevant
A loud and raucous din

'A Notation' is just a simple statement of frustration. I'm getting better at writing, but trying to convey the emotions from the mind, what there is of it, to the paper so others can find it is…oh, what was the word…. uh 'iffy'!

'Limericks' are fun to write, but you have to picture it first and then put it to paper; there we go with the iffy stuff again. I don't know anyone who can tell me if I have a ballpark's chance in he….if I'm doing it right, but I have to be close…?

A Notation

I can create a lovely thought
Emotions quite profound
But creation comes to naught
Should I write them down

I'll continue to try of course
With much vigor and élan
Though skills, iffy and coarse,
Suggest that I move on

Limerick

I knew a shirker named Larry
Who was a drunk and quite merry
One night a big score
His face met the floor
And now he drinks only dairy

haiku

bluebirds in the trees
sing sweetly in the spring rains
I left the top down

It is better to remain silent and be thought a fool than to speak out and remove all doubt.
~ Abraham Lincoln ~

Great ideas and excellent solutions to the world's ills have been created on this one ceramic monument. A monument to the creative juices (and others) that flow from a focused mind, although there may be times when the focus shifts just a bit. I have answered many of life's questions squa…..uh perched regally on the throne.

Pondering

I sit and ponder on the bathrone
The way things ought to be
A royal decree to shape and hone
For repairing domain wrongs

I create a lot of my best thinking
While squatting there alone
So many thoughts there forming
There the best are groan...grown

The free flowing chain of thought
Is sometimes uncontrolled
The streaming is randomly fraught
With an odious overflow

I struggle to render a proper work
At least that is my goal
Sometimes there's a costive break
That is truly bowled...bold

Squirming on my ceramic throne
To dislodge a fervid thought
But all I got was a painful bruise
And another way to squat

I sit and ponder on the bathrone
The way things ought to be
But the pressure on my backbone
Restricts good cogent flow

I have known since I was..5, or 6 that God existed; that He was. Back in the day I believed that God had done His job and that I was on my own. It took many years and a lot of mistakes to wake up to the fact that He had never been away. There were too many times when I made a choice to go one way and found myself headed in another. There is a saying that God protects drunks and fools. Well, having been both I can testify that, at least for me the saying is true. I can still be a fool. At least I recognize it.

The Light at the end

I've mostly had control pushing at my life
In whatever direction I chose
The choices, some good, tawdry and rife
Some really bad God knows

Every day brought a new enticing choice
And I had a taste of most
I celebrated all of it until I lost any choice
And my life began to coast

The upside was that the party never ends
And I enjoyed a good wallow
The downside was that I lost good friends
And my life was really hollow

Even while I waded through a host of it
There was a Presence there
His presence kept me from the worst of it
By directing me elsewhere

Later on I drifted slowly toward the light
A sluggish weighted travel
For me to find the path that was right
Evil ties needed to unravel

Now I can sit and ponder my bumpy path
And what I was guilty of
The times I should have felt God's wrath
And I only felt His love

The first few months of my retirement were anything but being cast adrift. Signing up for social security, Medicare and realigning my meager finances. The 'best' part was discovering all the information about both SS and Medicare that I had no clue about.

The first few months were almost as hard as still being at work…..now? Do I want to get up in the morning; if I do…do what?

Do I need to go….no. I should…yes, but maybe later. You get the idea. Nice!

Cast Adrift

Days slowly drift by both pallid and sere
Like the dust stirred by a vagrant breeze
An attenuating sound moving to the rear
Leaving a soft echo; a memory's tease

A stream of days each a mirror of the last
With an occasional spark, a tenuous glitch
So quickly come and just as quickly passed
Slide into obscurity without any real hitch

Back before my retirement held any sway
When memories were still being created
There was no singular need to find a way
To fill the hours as my time was saturated

Days flowed by so much faster back then
So early started and so quickly then done
A round trip commute and start it again
A tedious, vexatious and repetitive run

Whether working full tilt, or at a full rest
Days disappear and no dawdling, or pause
Remarks on their passing would be in jest
And any remarking is just flapping the jaws

Oh, what shall I do on this beautiful day
Read a good book, or indulge in a nap
Dwell in a new land, or let my mind stray
Either one will do with two cats in my lap

It has been a while and it is still very hard to talk about, much less write about. I have written on this subject a number of times and it never gets any easier. She was taken by some very careless hands and left an emptiness. She was removed from this world, 12/08/2004, by some arrogant, haughty.......good bye Kerri

Hollow Places

Sometimes as the day begins to die
And the others leave
A stark loneliness, hollowness, a sigh
And I began to grieve

Held at bay by strangers and friends
Alone there's no defense
And the greatest gift until night ends
Is my losing every sense

A friend introduced us in God's house
And she became my wife
The uncaring tore her from our house
And empty became my life

There is still a lingering, aching grief
A hollow place in my soul
The time we had was way too brief
A short time to be whole

An empty place; echoes of laughter
Can still elicit some pain
In the years that have come after
Echoes are on the wain

Day dawns slowly in streamers of red
Shreds of passing night
some of the saddest days have fled
but not all; not quite

It's amazing what two little lives can do to the cavernous structure that used to be a home. I do have to watch where I step because they are fast and quiet, and I have moved one or the other in a direction they had not chosen to go. It's also true that I am their butler and they own the place.

Little Stalkers

Feral shadows flow through the night
Weaving a sinuous path
And any trace of their passage is slight
A soft ripple in the dark

Tic-tac repeats on the hardwood floor
Betraying all of the stealth
Shredded furniture bleeds its padding
They're spreading the wealth

Floating dust motes create a distraction
Redirecting their focus
They are but a short term attraction
All too soon forgotten

A floor board creeks in another room
And they stop and stare
Then they stalk the unknown source
But there is nothing there

I need to watch where I put my feet
To avoid the little stalkers
Not always stealthy, but totally fleet
Appearing without notice

They fill many of the empty spaces
With warmth as they roam
Two cats residing; I am their butler,
Make this house a home

I studied for this one a lot. A sonnet should be a passionate display of couplets and quatrains extolling the love, or hate of a certain subject. I got the structure down, using Shakespeare's sonnets as a template I managed to crash and burn often. This is the third...no fourth rendition and there are only four as I had to stop because I was getting a headache. I will put neither of us through this again. So, enjoy this unique and purely hedonistic (?) pleasure.

A Sonnet

I'm blinded by the light that shines from you
Awash in warmth that permeates my heart
I'm buoyed by just the mere thought of you
Each night I'm hollow when you must depart

And yet it's not enough; I need you there
But there's a part of you inside that's cold
Is there a part of you that you can share?
Is there a way to reach the part on hold?

Together we can make this work, I'm sure
So, please reach out with open heart my dear
Of hate and painful enmity, we must abjure
The love together we can find is near

As long as I have breath enough to speak
True love from you is that, that I shall seek

Limerick

There was a cute girl from Dorsett
Who wore a cumbersome corset
She essayed to doff
It wouldn't come off
The only way was to force it

I'm never sure if I actually
have free time, or if I just
keep forgetting stuff
~ Anonymous ~

If I laid the book out right, you should have labored through uh... experienced 'a Sonnet' and been mesmerized by the eloquence and the...uh...pathos (?). The Bard would have been repel...appal......sigh! Anyway, there is a great epic poem just before this one that you should toss...uh...peruse and enjoy! (?)

Accidence

Sometimes an urge to create with words will emerge
An idea will appear that makes no sense at first see
It was a sonnet this time for my great primal urge
I should have bowed to the Bard and just let it be

So, I read the directions and I followed each word
I chased the instructions across more than one ream
As I chased and grammared everything just blurred
I persevered though my lack of training was extreme

First on the list was; look it up and define a quatrain
With the definition read a lot of confusion spread
I tripped hard on some couplets as I tried to retrain
Any chances of a sonnet were well and truly dead

It all began well enough and on such a high note
When the words and phrases all began to align
As I laid it down it brought a lump to my throat
And I was close to the title that I had to assign

At some vague point amidst all this enduing time
A kernel of, 'What?!', began to work its way out
It was making no sense and I choked on the rhyme
Because my train of thought had early dropped out

Well, I have finished whatever it was that I started
And the headache it gave me is on the way out
I'm pleased that this struggle and I have now parted
And now it is my time, oh, and a large glass of stout
.......or two

Some time ago I took a shot at writing a Limerick. It was fun so I wrote some more and then I decided to do a little writing outside the box and this poem was born. I do not apologize for taking a shot at the libtard.... liberal side of the political spectrum. All's fair in .... and war. Well, not *all*, but you get the idea.

A Linear Progress

I once saw a democrat work
At listing the work he would shirk
He babbled and drooled
With bourbon was fueled
Accomplished it all with a smirk

As he sat for a time to ponder
In a light formaldehyde haze
Falsehoods began to wander

And when the smug liberal lied
The others just took it in stride
He mumbled a line
Then started to whine
And let equilibrium slide

He carefully wobbled outside
As his eyes began to glaze over
He missed a step in his stride

I saw the same democrat fall
As he conversed with the wall
He told it to stop
He sat with a plop
While babbling loudly to all

Haiku

High dancing squirrel
Tightrope on telephone line
Frosty endeavor

So, in my never ending effort to write an epitaph on my inability to write let it be said here and now that I….. wrote this. I've written so many of these that I, on some occasion, should put together a section on gaffs, excuses and blank spaces. As a well qualified and experienced…??

Writer I am…uh..I am what? Uh…sigh!

Paradigm

This poem has its reason
It will have great rhyme
This poem will be perfect
So crisp and so sublime

This poem has a reason
This poem has a rhyme
This poem will be pleasin'
It's working out just fine

There's this fuzzy reason
I wanted this to rhyme
Choose a new direction
Or do I need more time?

Once there was a reason
I'm tanking on the rhyme
But maybe it's flu season
That has me off my mark

This poem had a reason
needed awesome rhyme
But I forgot the reason
Don't know how to rhyme

haiku

heavy clouds, hard tears
hail blasting murky puddles
ripples mingle; die

CPSIA information can be obtained
at www.ICGtesting.com
Printed in the USA
FSHW021851270620
71609FS

9 781796 068689